God's
Miracle
Child

The Britney Foster Story

Sherry Tatum knows how to pray-really pray! When her seven year old daughter Britney's life was at risk due to a horrible accident, Sherry went into full gear praying and fasting for fourteen days until God released the healing miracle. Within the pages of this book, Sherry takes the reader through her journey of miraculous faith trusting that Britney would live against all odds. Sherry believed that God would heal and restore her child. What a testimony of the goodness of God!

-Ann Platz: author

God's Miracle Child

The Britney Foster Story

Next to the Bible this is one of the truest stories you'll ever read.

By: Sherry Foster Tatum
Co-Written with: Thomas Reed

WestBow Press books may be ordered through booksellers or by contacting:

WestBow Press
A Division of Thomas Nelson
1663 Liberty Drive
Bloomington, IN 47403
www.westbowpress.com
1-(866) 928-1240

ISBN: 978-1-4497-1366-9 (sc)
ISBN: 978-1-4497-1367-6 (hc)
ISBN: 978-1-4497-1365-2 (e)

Library of Congress Control Number: 2011923434

All scripture quotations are taken from the King James Version of the Bible.

Printed in the United States of America

WestBow Press rev. date: 07/29/2011

To contact Sherry and Britney for a speaking engagement, please write them at:
P.O. Box 960
Kennesaw, GA 30156

Dedication

From Sherry —

I dedicate this book to —

The Lord Jesus – May I always tell the story of His love, mercy, grace and healing power. We know for a fact He is who the Bible and history says He is — The Savior of the world, God's only begotten Son — Who died for the sins of all the world for all people.

To Roy – My wonderful husband who is my soul mate and my biggest cheerleader. His words are like apples of gold in frames of silver. You will always have my love and respect. You are truly a man of God who loves me unconditionally. You've made my life happy and complete! God saved the best for last.

To my mother, Helen Marie – How can I ever thank you enough for all your fervent prayers, your constant presence and limitless faith when Britney and I needed you the most, and for your financial help. I love you Mom.

To my Aunt Bobbie – Whose quite strength and presence helped me to keep going. (I love you 2 much, 2 much!)

To my daughters Mistee and Holly – Who were only nine and five years old when Britney had the accident — You were such strong little women in such a hard-hard time. I know God heard your sweet prayers for your sister Britney. How I love you both.

To pastor Sammy Manus and Jimmy and Peggy Ledbetter – Thank you for your encouragement and financial help to have Britney's book republished. I couldn't have done it without you. Ya'll are my dearest friends.

From Britney—

I would like to take this opportunity to thank Mom and my sister Holly for all their many hours of baby-sitting for Caleb and Leigha, when I was trying to finish college.

To Mom, Roy, my sister Mistee, my sister Holly and Granny Honey — For their prayers and continued support. I love each of you so very much.

To my precious husband Chris — Who has always loved me just as I am — Who is a wonderful husband, father to our two children and my best friend. I will always love and respect you.

To all the many people I will never meet — Thank you from the bottom of my heart for praying and fasting for a little seven-year-old girl most of you didn't even know. When we all get to heaven I'll know you then and thank you personally. Until then, may the Lord bless and keep you all.

To my Dad Mike — Thanks for being so strong when I needed you most. I love you!

A Word of Thanks

I wish to thank all my family for their understanding and patience during our time of trial and for encouraging me to write this book about Britney.

Thanks to the many hundreds of people who prayed and fasted around the clock for Britney. I've never met you but I love you.

Thanks to Britney's Dad and my former husband, Mike Foster – his love and devotion to Britney was constant and without measure.

Thanks a trillion times over to Thomas Reed. Without him this book would never have been written. He helped me to pen my thoughts and put them on paper. He is a wonderful co-writer and friend.

Many, many thanks to Philip Deloach who was so kind to sketch the scenes in my book. He was a blessing and is a wonderful friend to me.

Foreword

To Britney –

Every time I celebrate a birthday with you I'm reminded that instead of celebrating another year of life with you, if not for God's healing power I could be putting flowers on a small grave. How great and kind is our heavenly Father — the Lord God.

Britney and her family live in Waleska, Georgia, a small town just outside Atlanta. At the time of the accident, she was seven years old. Mistee, Britney's older sister, was nine and Holly was five.

Foreword
by Samuel Manus

I believe *God's Miracle Child* gives an excellent display of God's divine intervention because of Sherry Tatum's prayers and obedience.

You will be thrilled as you see the Lord orchestrating the events that brought Britney from the jaws of death.

Several years ago when I met Roy, Sherry Tatum, and their family, I was greatly impressed with the testimony of Sherry and Britney. I could see how Sherry was compelled to fast and pray. She constantly called on the Lord with her prayers and supplication for Britney. Through her persistent prayers and obedience there came the manifestation of God's healing touch to Britney.

It is evident today of the grace and miracle power God has performed in Britney's life. Britney has given her testimony locally and in other countries.

Roy and Sherry have exemplified the Lord through their walk with God in ministry with television and teaching in many countries.

It is a tremendous joy to recommend this book for your encouragement. I can make this recommendation on my personal knowledge of the author.

Samuel Manus, Pastor
Victory Fellowship Church
Marietta, Georgia

Preface

We do not claim to understand all of God's supernatural ways. Nor do we advocate that He heals us only if we follow a set of prescribed rules of behavior. God's grace is not conditional; we do not earn His favor by our good works. But this one thing we do know: that whereas Britney was dying, now she lives.

Table of Contents

Chapter	Title	Page
1	That Tragic Saturday	1
2	Flesh of My Flesh	7
3	Can This Be Human?	13
4	The Battle for Britney	17
5	Job's Comforters	23
6	From Crises Come Blessings	27
7	Comfort in Tribulation	35
8	The Battle Resumes	39
9	God Remembered Us	47
10	The Valley of Depression	63
11	On the Mountain Top	71
12	After the Battle	75

1

That Tragic Saturday

"Mommy, Mommy, Britney's dead!" Holly, my youngest daughter, screamed as she darted across our front yard. Just then my neighbor, Bessie Campbell, broke through the tall underbrush separating our houses. Racing into my yard, she screamed, "Sherry, it's Britney. I think she's dead!"

"Britney . . . dead!" The words reverberated in my mind, then exploded filling my heart with fear. I couldn't think. Yet, my instincts continued to function; I heard myself ask questions I didn't really want answered — "Where's my baby? What happened?"

"She's at my house; Gary's trying to revive her. I called for an ambulance but it's not here — you'd better drive!"

As I sped around the block, my mind raced too. Britney's face flashed in front of me, her warm brown eyes, the wide grin. I imagined her as I had left her only minutes earlier — sprawled in front of the television watching Saturday morning cartoons. Then I imagined her cut or crushed; I could see her fragile frame mangled under Bessie's car. I prayed that this was all just a bad dream.

A nightmare couldn't have jolted me more than the scene at Bessie's. Near a pile of old railroad crossties, Britney lay. She wasn't moving. Blood from her nose and forehead soaked her hair. Gary, Bessie's husband, crouched over Britney with his ear pressed against her mouth. "He's listening for breath," I thought. "Oh, Lord, she is dead!"

1

When he saw me, Gary scooped Britney up and shot to his feet. "Sherry, a crosstie fell on her head. We'd better rush her to the hospital right now — she's barely breathing. Get in the back seat and hold Britney — I'll drive."

As Gary flew past cars, I clutched Britney's limp body to my chest. Spurts of hot air on my neck said she was alive; streams of warm blood on my shoulder said she was dying. Horrified, I screamed prayer; I pleaded with God to let her live. I pleaded with Britney to keep breathing.

But she didn't — just over halfway, she stopped. I gasped as if my own breath would revive her, then yelled, "Gary, she's dead — she's not breathing!"

"Breathe for her! Do CPR!" He insisted.

"I can't do it; I don't know how!"

"Listen! You'd better do exactly what I say right now or she'll die!"

Gary's sternness pushed me beyond the normal bounds of my capabilities. Following his instructions, I forced a quick puff of air into Britney's mouth and then pressed on her chest. Twice I repeated this life-giving process. After forcing Britney to exhale the third time, she gasped; she was breathing again.

Gary drove even faster now. The highway patrol tried to stop us but Gary didn't even slow down; instead he motioned toward Britney and me in the back seat. When the law officers saw us, they pulled ahead and, with sirens wailing and lights flashing, escorted us to Kennestone Hospital in Marietta.

There, as I handed Britney to an orderly, the sight of her bloody head and limp body overwhelmed me and I fainted. When I awoke — some five minutes later — I was in a wheel-chair against a wall in the emergency unit.

The doors flew open and my husband, Mike, burst through: "I don't care what you do, but somebody please help my baby — she's dying!" From nurse to nurse he shifted, begging for information on Britney's condition, but there was none.

Everyone buzzed around the emergency room ignoring Mike. Not to be denied, he grabbed Dr. Barnett, the attending physician, by the shirt and held him. "I don't care what it takes, just make Britney well! You can have our house and anything we own. Please, make her stay alive!"

Mike looked surprised when Dr. Barnett replied, "Mr. Foster, I'd do my best to save your daughter's life even if you didn't have a dime to your name."

Following an examination, Dr. Barnett, a neurosurgeon, diagnosed a severe concussion. Britney was comatose but she was taken to a room in the Children's Wing to recover, no special treatment was prescribed. Dr. Barnett told us she'd probably go home in a couple of days.

The initial shock was past; our fears were now replaced by hope. I called home to share the good news. Mistee, Britney's older sister, finally answered, but she could hardly talk; her voice trembled. Yet, she managed to explain what had happened to Britney.

While I had gone for a newspaper and while Mike painted the house, Mistee and her sisters played with the neighborhood twins, Aimee and Amanda. They were so preoccupied with their games that, when Mike ran out of paint, he left them while he went for more.

As he hopped into the van, Mike explained to Mistee, "I'll be right back. Now, you look out for Britney and Holly while I'm gone."

Then, as he backed out of the driveway, he yelled out the window, "Go over to Gary's and ask him if he'll help me bring some crossties over to our house when I get back."

Mistee misunderstood what her dad said; she thought he wanted the girls to get the crossties while he was gone. Although railroad crossties weigh nearly two hundred pounds, Mistee was determined to obey her father; she knew he wanted them to make borders around flower beds in our yard.

So, off went my girls with the twins. As they did, Britney insisted that Mistee was wrong, that their dad didn't want them to carry those heavy crossties. Mistee's interpretation prevailed.

Gary was asleep so Mistee beat on his front door until he awoke. She explained her plans and Gary, still half asleep and knowing the girls couldn't carry a crosstie by themselves, nodded his approval. He then went back to sleep and the five little girls proceeded with their project.

Having a measure of success, they managed to raise one crosstie to a vertical position. Together they had stood that extremely heavy mass of wood on its end, a process they planned to repeat as they "walked" the crosstie over to our house.

Then tragedy struck! Holly and the twins decided they had had enough so they left Mistee and Britney to finish the job alone. Overwhelmed by the heavy weight, Mistee fell back onto Gary's pickup truck. Britney also succumbed, but she fell onto the pile of crossties face down with her forehead resting on the corner of one. Before Britney could move, the crosstie crashed down onto the back of her head driving deep into her skull and brain on the right side. Though the damage was severe, as we later learned, it was not apparent under Britney's long hair. More noticeable was a deep laceration on her forehead where her head had been driven into the crosstie which lay on the ground.

Mistee thought Britney was dead but she had enough presence of mind to summon help. She screamed and beat on Gary's windows and doors until she woke him again. When he came to the door, Mistee could not talk; she could only point at her sister. Gary sprang out of the house, ran to Britney and, with a surge of adrenalin, lifted the crosstie off her head. He then began frantically checking to see if she were still alive; she was, but just barely. Britney was not breathing, her color was gone, her pupils were dilated, and she had swallowed her tongue. Her only life sign was a faint pulse. She lay deathly still.

4

Gary was unsure of what to do at first. Based on his observations of Vietnam war victims, he thought Britney would die no matter what he did. So he ruled out CPR. But then he changed his mind. Thank God he did because he managed to get Britney breathing on her own.

Mistee had already run home and shut herself in her bedroom closet where she remained until I telephoned. For five hours she screamed and cried. She pleaded with God — "Why did this happen to Britney of all people? Why did you allow me to hurt her this way? Lord, please let her live — take my life and let Britney live!"

To comfort Mistee, I told her that Britney was all right, that she'd be home in a few days. But she couldn't accept this — etched in her brain was a picture of Britney's bloody head crushed between two massive pieces of wood. This sight and the thought that she was responsible tormented Mistee and would continue to haunt her for many months.

She was not alone in her agony. Saturday night as we waited in Britney's room, Mike, too, had feelings of guilt. He blamed himself for having left the girls alone those few fateful minutes.

I, too, felt guilty because I thought God was getting even with me for my spiritual condition. For nearly fourteen years I had failed God and now He was making me pay. I felt Britney was suffering because of me.

Yet, I felt powerless to help her even through prayer. I believed in God and the power of prayer; but, since the age of nineteen, I had not served Him as I should. Fearing that God would not answer my prayers now, I turned to my mother for help.

God would hear Mother; He had answered her prayers before. Many times, He had manifested Himself in her life, even with healing miracles. In the weary days ahead, Mother would stand as a pillar of strength and a rock I could lean on.

Saturday night gave us an indication of what we had in store in the days to come. Britney's condition worsened as the night wore on. Her head swelled and blood oozed from her nostrils. Her eyes darkened and swelled shut. She gritted her teeth and chewed her tongue causing it to bleed and swell. Her breathing became extremely labored.

The nurses reassured us that they were doing all they could for our daughter. We wanted more. We felt that the doctors needed to examine Britney again, but throughout the night, they didn't and her condition continued to deteriorate. As her condition worsened, our earlier hope vanished. We now had no assurance that Britney would live through the night.

2

Flesh of My Flesh

Early Sunday morning, a new nurse for the day shift complied with Mike's request to call Dr. Barnett. His subsequent examination of Britney produced more attention for her in a span of ten minutes than she had received throughout the entire night. Additional X-rays were hurriedly taken; this time, the back of her head was included.

After reviewing the X-rays, Dr. Barnett ordered immediate surgery. The back of Britney's skull was crushed, driving bone fragments into her right cerebellum, severely damaging this portion of her brain. In addition her skull was cracked all the way around with hundreds of hairline fractures extending off the major fracture. The swelling had progressed to the point that, according to Dr. Barnett, Britney's life depended on surgery.

Time was of the essence; doctors and nurses buzzed around her room. Following hastily completed preparations, at 11:30 on Sunday morning, Britney was taken into surgery.

Before Dr. Barnett darted into the operating room, he imparted more bad news. "Britney's in the deepest comatose state possible. Administering anesthesia for surgery will mean putting her in an even deeper sleep. I'll do all I can but it doesn't look good."

During the four hours Britney was in surgery, I did a great deal of soul-searching. I could not dismiss the thought that

Britney was dying because of my slackness toward God. As I reflected on my life, I was saddened by my failure to serve Him as I should.

I thought of the sweetness of my experience when God saved me at the age of fourteen. My heart was tender and the infilling of God's Spirit blessed me with peace and spiritual happiness. God's presence was real to me during this time as I prayed, fasted, and studied His Word incessantly. His power was real to me, too, as, on several occasions, He manifested Himself with miracles. I served God through high school, but shortly after graduation, I moved away from home and my convictions weakened. Filled with zest for living, I wanted to be free to do things like my friends. I felt deprived because I wouldn't allow myself to live. My life was going by and all I did was watch everybody else doing things I wanted to do. I felt like an outsider — a fifth wheel. Nothing good was being produced in my life and that saddened me.

Because I believed in strict compliance with God's laws, I began to envision Him as a hard taskmaster with a whip who eagerly strikes us down every time we make a mistake. Since I felt that all I did was make mistakes, I thought, "What's the use? I'm a failure. God doesn't want someone like me around." I even began to believe He didn't love me and that I was of no importance to Him. A disabling fear of not being the perfect Christian constantly tormented me. Since I had been taught that God expects nothing less than perfection — and I was far from perfect — I saw no need to continue serving the Lord; I was seeking an unattainable goal.

Just once I wish someone had come along and told me that God loved me unconditionally and that since I was a "babe in Christ," I should not give up. I should keep trying, learn by my mistakes and grow in the Lord. But no one ever came.

My continued service for God seemed futile. Finally, I grew weary of struggling. Unable to take the constant pressure of not knowing how to serve God, I quit trying. And when I did, I lived as I pleased.

Mike and I were married about three years after I gave up on God. Soon there were children — three precious girls. We loved them dearly.

Quite by accident, at the age of twenty-nine, I got into acting and landed parts in several movies and numerous commercials. Still there was something missing; a miserable void that I couldn't fill pervaded my being. The applause, the recognition, the money never seemed to satisfy and make me completely happy. The inner peace I craved was not mine. Gone was the vital spark which burned in my soul when God was given His rightful place in my life.

Even though I had turned my back on God, my thoughts frequently drifted to Him and the sweetness of my salvation experience. I still loved and feared God and knew I needed to change. I longed to return to Him as a wayfaring daughter longs for her father. But for nearly fourteen years, I refused to commit my life back to Him.

I resisted the continual tug of the Holy Spirit because I didn't think I could live as God required. I reasoned, "I just can't go back trying to serve the Lord. That's a big commitment. I'd want to keep it and, right now, I don't know how. I don't want to fail Him again. I can't keep all the laws of the Old Testament." At that time in my life I did not know Jesus had freed us from the law of Moses.

I stayed heartbroken. I still thought I wasn't good enough for God. I even thought that maybe He didn't know me after all. Yet, deep down, I hoped that someday God would show Himself to me in such a way that proved He loved me and that help was on the way. Help never came.

Now, confronted by the possible loss of my child, fourteen years of failure stared me in the face. There could be no more excuses; I desperately needed God now. I recalled the

Scripture dealing with "the destruction of the flesh, that the spirit may be saved" (1 Corinthians 5:5). I related the Apostle Paul's admonition of one who had committed a deplorable act to my own spiritual inadequacies. Was God going to destroy Britney — my flesh — to save my soul?

I didn't want that so I pleaded with God, "You don't have to take Britney to bring me back. That's not necessary, Lord. I'll come back to You. I've always wanted to live for You; I just didn't know how. I still don't know how, but if You'll help me I'll do the best I can. Just forgive me of my sins and accept me back, Lord."

I committed myself totally to serve God; the method of service was unimportant. My fourteen-year-old excuse of not knowing how to properly serve God was discarded and replaced by determination to serve Him by the method of His choosing. Britney Foster, flesh of my flesh, was reason enough — if I needed a reason — to do my best to please God.

Now, when I reflect on this decision to serve God, I realize how foolish I was for thinking that God didn't love me. God is love and He loved me before the foundations of the world — " . . . I have loved thee with an everlasting love" (Jeremiah 31:33). Even before I knew Him, He knew me on an intimate basis and loved me with unending, unconditional love — "According as he hath chosen us in him before the foundation of the world, that we should be holy and without blame before him in love" (Ephesians 1:4). I now realize that I was important enough for Him to continue looking for and drawing me back to Him. Yes, I would try to please God, for He is worthy.

Having reviewed my life and made my decision to commit all to God, my spirits were uplifted. The redemptive power of the blood of Christ had been reapplied to my heart and the peace I had craved for nearly half my life was finally mine.

In harmony with the Spirit of God once again, my thoughts returned to Britney. I knew that God's grace looks at our helplessness rather than our worthiness but in my despair I linked my spirituality with Britney's condition. I therefore questioned whether my commitment to God had been in time. Had I conveniently excused myself for too long from His perfect will, or would God let Britney live in spite of my slackness toward Him?

3

Can This Be Human?

Around 4:00 Sunday afternoon, Dr. Barnett came from surgery to the waiting room. With a grim face he explained that the surgery had involved the opening of Britney's skull to expose her brain. A large piece of bone and several bone fragments were extracted from her brain and, in the process, a portion of the cerebellum was excised. Finally, a blood clot the size of an egg yolk was removed from her brain.

Dr. Barnett then explained the condition of Britney's brain. The blood clot had caused extensive damage as it had starved surrounding cells of vital nutrients. Having hemorrhaged throughout the night, her brain had swollen to capacity; so much so that he feared it would "pop like popcorn" before he completed the surgery. He further pointed out that the force of the blow to Britney's head had caused severe trauma to most of her cerebellum — it was "scrambled like jelly." As a result, the right side of Britney's body was paralyzed.

Her general condition was not much better. Dr. Barnett talked about Britney's inability to breathe on her own and of the need for a total life support system. Special nurses would be assigned to britney in the Intensive Care Unit; around the clock care was a necessity.

The outlook was bleak at best — Dr. Barnett offered little hope. He didn't even give Britney a fifty/fifty chance of making it through the night. When I asked him if she were going to die, he just shook his head. "She may not make it. I've done all that man can do for Britney. If you know God, I suggest you go pray for your daughter. She's now in the hands of a higher power than mine."

"Dr. Barnett, I have been praying for Britney and I'll continue to pray for her." Prayer was all I had to offer; a bout with walking pneumonia forced me to remain outside Britney's room.

I felt helpless What could I do when Dr. Barnett himself had turned her over to a higher power? The answer lay outside my own abilities; I must place my total dependence on this higher power of which Dr. Barnett spoke. With a heavy heart, I cried out to Him, "Lord, I'm depending on You to save Britney's life — You're the only one who can help her. The doctors have done all they can and I can't even go in to see her."

Unable to be with my baby, I would stand on a foot stool in the hall and gaze at her in the ICU through a small window. Seeing her thrash about with tubes in her nose, IV's in her arms, and an EKG monitor attached to her chest was almost unbearable. The weight of my sorrow threatened to crush me; my heart ached to be with Britney, to touch her. I'd think, "God, what if she dies? The next time I touch her, she'll be dead."

That Sunday night, Britney looked as if she might die. Her head resembled a huge pear — it had swollen more at the top, almost as large as a basketball — with no human features evident. Her nose had disappeared, her eyes had swollen shut, and her lips had stretched almost to the point of bursting. The laceration on her forehead gapped open as it remained unstitched.

The sight of Britney's head, distorted beyond recognition, was nauseating. My cousin fainted when she saw her. Someone even thoughtlessly asked, "Can this be human?"

Britney's grave condition and grotesque appearance were the realization of my most dreaded fear. As I looked at her through the little ICU window, I thought how that all her life Mike and I had worried about her. We had an inexplicable feeling that if anything ever happened to one of the girls, it would be to Britney.

Adversity seemed to follow her. Even before she was born, she had problems — in my second month of pregnancy with her, I nearly miscarried; in the seventh month, I almost hemorrhaged to death. Just to bring Britney into the world, an emergency caesarean section had to be performed. She was born with yellow jaundice and for months she always seemed to be sick. She had had double pneumonia twice by her fourth birthday.

She was a beautiful baby though. She had silky smooth skin and big brown eyes highlighted by long black eyelashes.

Somewhat timid, Britney was not as outgoing and rambunctious as her sisters. Yet, she seemed to be at peace with herself. Her spirit could best be described as quiet, sweet, and easygoing.

Britney was a loving child too. Flowers from the yard, love notes, and colorful drawings presented to her dad and me were expressions of that love. And the motherly way she cuddled and cared for her baby sister further indicated her compassion.

But outside her family, Britney's love often went unnoticed because she hid her true feelings from others. As she was less outgoing than Mistee and Holly, other children tended to shun Britney and she, in turn, withdrew from them. She developed into somewhat of a loner, always remaining in the background. Though it saddened her, she never complained about her role. And she didn't force herself on others to attract the attention she deserved.

Because Britney was the underdog and because other kids shied away from her, Mike and I were prompted to fill the gap by showering her with our love. Mike was especially partial to "his precious." Yet, she had a strong need to cling to me — a need I attributed to her inability and unwillingness to fend for herself.

Both Mike and I sensed this weakness in Britney and compensated by constantly protecting her. We felt compelled to stand guard over her and, when we couldn't, we cautioned her incessantly.

In spite of our love and our passion for Britney's safety, she now lay at the point of death — the victim of an accident we had been powerless to prevent. Young and innocent, Britney had been totally unsuspecting of the tragedy that befell her. Now, it appeared that she would be denied an opportunity to experience the hopes, the happiness, and even the disappointments associated with growing up.

Britney was miraculously still alive and we were thankful to God. For her to remain alive, the war of faith — trusting God rather than dwelling on the obstacles facing her — had to be waged. And interceding for Britney, even battling for her life, became my way of life in the weary days ahead.

4

The Battle For Britney

From my teenage experience with God, I knew that He whom I had committed to serve was a healer of man's diseases — "But he was wounded for our transgressions, he was bruised for our iniquities; the chastisement of our peace was upon him, and with his stripes we are healed" (Isaiah 53:5). He is a God "who healeth all thy diseases" (Psalms 103:3).

And I knew that God still healed people, even in our day. As I sat in the hospital chapel, I devoured brochures and booklets on healing. In them I read accounts of individuals who had been healed by the power of God. Their inspirational testimonies made me wonder what, if anything, God required of me before He would heal my daughter. I didn't know, but for Britney's sake I was determined to find out and then, to the best of my ability, do it.

The first thing I did was to ask God to keep away the death angel and send Britney a ministering angel. I felt that He honored my request because each time I approached Britney's room, I could see, in my mind's eye, a huge angel standing at her door with his sword poised in a vertical position in front of his face.

Then I proclaimed a fast. I promised God, "I will not eat a bite of food until I eat with Britney. When she eats, I will eat!" Though I didn't link fasting with healing, I wanted to show God how serious I was about Britney's healing. And I remembered that God, in His Word, advocates that we fast — "But thou, when thou fastest, anoint thine head, and wash thy face, That thou appear not unto men to fast, but unto thy Father, who is in secret and thy Father, who seeth in secret, shall reward thee openly" (Matthew 6:17, 18).

However, the presence of a ministering angel and the proclamation of a fast were not enough; for Britney's healing, I felt that more was needed. As I looked at her distorted head, I was convinced that we were in an impossible, no-win situation; if Britney lived — and this was doubtful — she would be disfigured for the rest of her life.

Mother was quick to point out that God often works in impossible situations to manifest His love and to keep His promises. She reminded me that God made a great nation out of Abraham in spite of what appeared to be an impossibility. Sarah was barren, both Abraham and Sarah were "old and well stricken in age," and Abraham had no land. Yet, Abraham heeded the call of God through faith.

I reasoned that healing could be mine (Britney's) if I were "fully persuaded" through faith to believe that, what God has promised, He is able also to perform. But how could I be sure I had enough faith for Britney's healing?

I turned to God's Word for help. I read and absorbed as much Scripture as I possibly could, at times even burying my face in the big, white Bible opened on the altar in the prayer room. I was determined to fill my mind, body, and soul with the words of my Heavenly Father.

As I studied, I began to realize that it was the Scriptures themselves that would develop and defend my faith — "Faith cometh by hearing, and hearing by the Word of God" (Romans 10:17). By knowing the Word, I could pray in agreement with the promises. And I would be better prepared to withstand the attacks of Satan. God's Word is our sword — Satan can't stand up to it. But, if he can stop us from studying the Bible and cling-

ing to the promises set forth therein, he has won half the battle.

Determined to deny Satan an advantage, I searched God's Word for instances of healing to increase my faith. I found many, but the one which comforted me the most was that of Jarius' daughter in the fifth chapter of Mark.

When I read these verses, hope pervaded my being; a little girl just like Britney had been healed. These life-giving words of Mark had such impact on me that I had Mike place a Bible, opened to the healing of Jarius' daughter, on Britney's bed and under no circumstances was it to be removed.

I was further consoled when, in my studies, I learned of Christ's continuing concern for the believer. What He did for Jairus' daughter, He could do for my child because He never changes — "Jesus Christ, the same yesterday, and today, and forever" (Hebrews 13:8). Even though Christ no longer ministers personally to man, He is still our High Priest — a compassionate high priest (Hebrews 4:15). And as our personal advocate with the Father, He is forever making intercession for the saints (Hebrews 7:25).

But He still wants us to "come boldly unto the throne of grace, that we may obtain mercy, and find grace to help in time of need" (Hebrews 4:16). So, Mother and I spent most of our time in the prayer room; we prayed almost continuously. If ever we needed grace to help in time of need, it was now. Britney needed to be healed and prayer was essential — "pray one for another, that ye may be healed. The effectual, fervent prayer of a righteous man availeth much" (James 5:16).

I also learned that along with faith and prayer, the child of God must be steadfast. In trials and tests — tools often used by God to mold and shape us into the Christians He wants us to be (1 Peter 1:7) — we must not waver (Hebrews 10:23). We must trust God and never doubt His willingness to deliver in any situation.

That deliverance takes many forms. Mother knew this and tried to prepare me by pointing out that God has a divine plan within His sovereign will for each Christian. For reasons known only to God Himself, some people are never healed. But many are — some are healed after seeking God many times, some are healed gradually, some are healed instantly.

As I wanted instant healing for Britney, I became impatient at times; I wanted God to move quickly. On one such occasion, after praying for hours with no results, I complained that God wasn't listening.

Again I was influenced by Mother's wisdom as she lectured me on trusting God — "Sherry, Christianity is much more than going to church. It is believing in God to the extent that our belief translates into trust — trust that He does hear our prayers and that He will provide for us in all of life's trials and tests. Dear, it's easy to say we trust God when everything's going our way. That's not all God wants. He expects us to look to Him and have confidence in Him in our time of need as well. God has promised to care for us and He cannot lie. If He promises healing in His Word — and He does — then healing is available. Remember that, Sherry. God can bring life out of death — He can heal Britney!"

This was my hope, my only hope. Only God could help us now so I clung to Him; I refused to release Him of His promises. Britney's life was at stake and I was determined to see her healed.

5

Job's Comforters

"Then Job answered and said, I have heard many such things. Miserable comforters are ye all. Shall vain words have an end? Or what emboldeneth thee that thou answerest? I also could speak as ye do. If your soul were in my soul's stead, I could heap up words against you, and shake mine head at you" (Job 16:1-4).

Although I trusted God to heal Britney, Satan would not concede defeat. Instead, he counterattacked by sending his "ambassadors of doom" to sow seeds of doubt. They did this under the guise of consoling and preparing me for Britney's inevitable death.

One day when Mother and I prayed, two of these "Job's Comforters" paid us a visit in the chapel. They began, as had others, by consoling me for the calamity which they felt would soon befall me. "Mrs. Foster, you should prepare yourself for the worst. If Britney dies, you need to be able to get hold of yourself and be in control for your other two children."

My righteous indignation was stirred. "If you don't have any more faith than that, please leave. Don't come in here giving me those tales because there's nothing but the Word of God in this room. Our minds are in one accord with the Lord and His Word. If you don't have any faith and you can't get down here and pray with us, don't bother telling me to prepare for my daughter's death. I don't believe God that way."

They attempted to calm me down. "Mrs. Foster, you're just hysterical. You need to get in control of yourself. You need to realize that God takes people and that people have to die."

"That's right, but you've got to realize that God's a healer too. God created Britney and if He wants to heal her, He can. I can console myself if I want to, but the Lord wants us to think on things that are pure and lovely. That's what I'm thinking on. To me, there's nothing any lovelier than when Jesus healed people."

They retaliated. "You've got to be willing to accept the will of the Lord."

I disagreed. "If the Word says I'm serving a God who heals all our diseases, should I pray, 'Lord, if it's Your will, heal Britney'? No, I shouldn't because it is His will to heal people. He's full of compassion; He loves to give His children good gifts. What better gift could God give me than the healing of my child? He said, 'According to your faith be it unto you' (Matthew 9:29). My faith is that He created her and He can heal her."

By then I was preaching. "You've got to remember, too, what God did for Hezekiah. God told Isaiah to go tell Hezekiah to get his house in order because he was going to die. Hezekiah turned his face to the wall and wept bitterly before the Lord and asked Him to spare his life. The Lord told Isaiah to go back and tell Hezekiah that He had heard his prayers and seen his tears and that He was going to give him fifteen more years to live.

"Now, if the Lord would spare Hezekiah, a grown man, is He not equally willing to spare the life of a little child? I'm a child of God, so He has to hear my prayers and see my tears just like He did Hezekiah's."

Our visitors were dumbfounded and speechless. They listened intently as I continued. "What argument can you have against 'with his stripes we are healed' and that God 'healeth all thy diseases'? What can you say to that? What if Jairus had come to Jesus and said, 'Lord, my little daughter lies at the point of death; but if it's Your will, let her die'? He didn't say that. He said, 'Lord, all You've got to do is just come to my house and I know she'll be all right.' Jesus didn't say, 'Oh, you're not in my will!' Instead, He said, 'Be not afraid, only believe.' "Where does faith come in? You people want to just say, 'Thy will be done' and forget it. Why? Because there's no faith involved, there's no holding on to God until He answers."

With that, I opened the door and asked our visitors to leave. Quite relieved to get away from me, they bustled out the door. They never came back.

No matter how hard they tried, "Job's Comforters" could not change my mind. My confidence was that a God who is big enough to put the stars in the heavens and who causes the sun to come up each morning could surely heal one little child. Instead of looking at the circumstances, I was trusting God to prevail and deliver Britney from her bed of affliction. This gave me peace of mind because I could rest in the assurance that God had everything under control and that, in His time and in His way, He would heal my baby.

"Thou wilt keep him in perfect peace, whose mind is stayed on thee, because he trusteth in thee. Trust ye in the Lord forever; for in the Lord Jehovah is everlasting strength" (Isaiah 26:3,4).

25

6

From Crises
Come Blessings

I believed God would heal Britney; yet she remained critically ill showing no signs of improving. For three days, we waited for a change in her condition but nothing happened. Then, on day four, the crises began. For seven days, Britney was assailed by one crisis after another — most life-endangering and all very real.

From the beginning, Britney couldn't seem to inhale deeply enough; each day, her breathing difficulties grew worse. Even with the respirator, her right lung barely expanded. We told the nurses that something was wrong with her lungs but, for three days, no one listened.

Then on the fourth day, Dr. Sessions, a respiratory specialist, ordered chest X-rays.

Mother and I were in the prayer room so he discussed his findings with Mike — "Mr. Foster, we took X-rays of Britney's lungs and I'm afraid the results are not at all encouraging."

A lump formed in Mike's throat. "Why, what's wrong?"

"Her right lung has a hole in it that's allowing air to escape. In fact, the X-rays show a huge pocket of air surrounding the lung. Now, to draw this air out of her body, we've got to surgically insert a tube through Britney's back and up to her lung. I don't know at this point what we'll do with the lung."

"Is there any way you could be wrong, Dr. Sessions? Britney's not strong enough for surgery."

"No, Mr. Foster. I'm afraid we'll need to insert the tube at once."

Shortly after Dr. Sessions left, Mother and I came up from the prayer room to see Britney. As I gazed at her through the little window, Mike walked up and stood beside me. I sensed a difference in him and when he told me the bad news, I cried, "What next? Britney can't take much more!"

Apparently the crosstie that crushed Britney's skull had burst her lung as well. As a result, she had lain for three days with only one lung functioning. Now we knew why her chest had not been expanding on the right side.

As Dr. Sessions would not elaborate on the planned course of treatment for this newest complication, we didn't know what to expect. However, when one of the nurses conveniently informed Mother that a person could live with only one lung, I knew they were considering the removal of Britney's right lung.

I couldn't accept this development; immediate action was needed. "Mother, let's go back to the prayer room. Britney can't stand to go back under anesthesia again. She's in such a weakened state and so near death that it might kill her this time."

In the prayer room, I sank to my knees in front of the small altar. My head was spinning and my body, which seemed on fire, trembled as I prayed. Everything within me cried out to God — "Your Word declares that You'll never leave us or forsake us and that You're with us when everyone else deserts us. Your Word tells me that You created Britney and that You have all power in heaven and earth. You said You were our healer, Father. So, please have mercy upon Britney and heal her lung. Let her live to ever praise and magnify Your name. Lord, I give her to You; Her life is Your hands. In Jesus' name I pray for this miracle. Amen."

With our spirits filled with the outpouring of God's love, and with complete faith in Him to bless us with our needed miracle, Mother and I went back upstairs. As we were stepping out of the elevator, Mike was running down the hall toward us. "There you are. I've been looking for you two. You won't believe this, but Dr. Sessions came back with another report. He had to take more X-rays to see where to put the tube in Britney's back. It's the strangest thing because now he can't find the hole in her lung. He can't find the air around the lung either. Dr. Sessions said they were both gone."

Mother and I beamed.

We were denied an opportunity to tell Mike of our prayers because he continued after pausing just long enough to take another deep breath. "I asked him, 'What do you mean, they're gone? Could all those X-rays have been wrong?' Dr. Sessions didn't have an answer for that. His only explanation was, 'I don't know what to tell you. All I know is that they're gone and we don't have to operate.'"

Mike was baffled. How could the X-rays be wrong? How could the hole in Britney's lung have suddenly disappeared without a trace?

God had given us our first miracle! Truly, His greatness is beyond human reason. He is the Lord God who has all majesty and all power. He created all life; He sustains all life. He heals the sick; for that I praise Him.

* * * *

Since the accident, Britney had extreme fluctuations in body temperature — a common malady among patients with severe brain damage. To combat the high fever, a cooling blanket was used. When Britney's fever reached dangerous levels, the blanket was turned on and in a matter of minutes, it would be icy cold.

Although the cold helped stabilize her body temperture, I hated for Britney to lie on that icy blanket. As she couldn't move, I imagined that she wanted me to cuddle her and make her warm and comfortable. But I couldn't — I wasn't allowed in her room.

On day six, Britney's fever went extremely high — in excess of 105 degrees. When it did, Mother and I returned to the chapel. Once again we asked God to move on Britney's behalf. Not only was the high fever damaging to her brain, but it meant that Britney had to remain on that dreadful cooling blanket.

God says in His Word that "we walk by faith, not by sight" (2 Corinthians 5:7). So I prayed, "Lord, help me to walk by faith. What I see seems so real and what the doctors say is so discouraging. Lord, hang on to me. Keep me strong during this test of faith. I know there is victory in Jesus. Your Word says He was victorious over death, Hell, and the grave. Father, I'm taking You at Your Word, for You cannot deny Yourself (2 Timothy 2:13). Lord, I'm asking You to heal Britney's fever so she can be taken off that icy cold blanket. In Jesus' name. Amen."

When we returned to Britney's room, the fever was gone. But, throughout the day it came and went. Our faith was being tested, but Mother and I held to our convictions. God had healed Britney's lung; He wouldn't fail us now.

And He didn't; He just had His own time. Early on day seven, Britney's fever subsided to a controllable level and, because it remained there, the cooling blanket was removed. I was relieved because now Britney wouldn't have to contend with the biting cold along with all her other problems. I thanked God for answering our prayers once again.

Also, on the seventh day, my bout with walking pneumonia ended and I was allowed to go into Britney's room. Even though I cherished the time with her, my heart was broken; she looked pitiful. I caught myself staring at her and, as I did, I visualized her as she was. I could see her black and swollen eyes — eyes that were once beautiful — opening and looking at me. I could see her puffy lips moving and saying, "Mommy, I'm going out to play. I'll be careful."

Her imprisonment continued, but I was at last free to touch and comfort Britney's frail body. I massaged her arms and legs and rubbed her toes. I stroked her hair and kissed her fingers and swollen face.

While I was loving Britney, Dr. Barnett came in. Sensing my joy, he too seemed excited. However, his excitement quickly turned to remorse. "Mrs. Foster, I've placed Britney on a drug called Dilantin — I don't know for how long. People like your daughter, with severe brain damage, have to be given this drug to keep them calm and to prevent seizures. Epilepsy and seizures are normally by-products of severe brain damage and we don't want that for Britney."

"Dr. Barnett, I don't want Britney on drugs the rest of her life either. Is this absolutely necessary?"

"Yes, I'm afraid it is. I'm sorry."

What my eyes saw and what my ears heard contradicted what I sensed in my spirit. Since I believed God was going to heal Britney, I felt He could take her off this medication as well. But I asked myself how Dr. Barnett could possibly know when to take her off the Dilantin; she remained comatose, so how would he know she no longer needed the drug?

I didn't know how but I knew who did. So I went to Him in prayer — "Lord, I don't want my child, who has been healed so many times to Your glory, to be on this medication. I don't want her to be sedated all her life unable to function to her full potential. Whatever You can do to get her off this Dilatin or any other drugs, please do it. Perform a miracle and let her be taken off this medication. In Jesus' name I pray. Amen."

All I could do then was wait on the Lord. "Wait on the Lord, be of good courage, and he shall strengthen thine heart. Wait, I say, on the Lord" (Psalms 27:14). Only He could deliver; there was no other way.

That evening, God began to move, but in a mysterious way; Britney broke out in a rash over her entire body. I realize that we are to walk by faith and not by sight, but this seemed to push me beyond the bounds of my faith. I complained to Mother — "I can't stand anything else. I can't take this. Britney keeps having so many things go wrong, and she looks horrible with that rash all over her body."

"Sherry, where would faith come from if we weren't tested, if everything came easy? Honey, you've got to believe that God determines the outcome in all situations. He loves us and He's bound by His promises."

In my haste to look at the circumstances, I failed to realize that God was answering prayer; the rash was a blessing in disguise. When Dr. Barnett saw it, he ordered the nurses to discontinue the use of Dilantin. God knew the way when there seemed to be no way.

The next day, day eight, the rash disappeared but yet another crisis had developed. When I went in to see Britney, I knew something was wrong by the sad look on the nurses' faces. When I asked why they were so disturbed, they ignored me; one even asked me to leave. But I would not be denied; I had to have an answer.

Finally, one young nurse told me, "Britney has a severe bladder infection. We're getting a lot of blood and pus in her urine." One look at the catheter tube and I knew why they were concerned.

Despair gripped me as I talked to God — "No, Lord! I can't hold on any longer. What else can I say? After all Britney has gone through, must she also suffer with a bladder infection?"

Mother felt my pain. "Sherry, come with me to the prayer room. I know you're tired, but come anyway; God will honor your effort."

I was so weak I couldn't pray. I just stretched on the floor in front of the altar and whispered, "Where can I run to in my day of trouble, to whom can I run for help? I will cry unto my God, my rock, my refuge, my very present help in the time of trouble. I will cry unto the Lord, the God of all flesh who said, 'Call unto me, and I will answer thee, and show thee great and mighty things, which thou knowest not' (Jeremiah 33:3)."

And He did show us great and mighty things; God supernaturally moved again, instantly. When Mother and I returned to Britney's room, the urine within the catheter tube was almost clear again — the bladder infection was gone!

What better faith builder than answered prayer! We were becoming more and more confident that no matter what the next crisis might be, God would hear and He would answer.

7

Comfort in Tribulation

"Blessed be God, even the Father of our Lord Jesus Christ, the Father of mercies, and the God of all comfort, who comforteth us in all our tribulation" (2 Corinthians 1:3, 4).

With each passing day, I became more fatigued. The crises, the constant vigil, the fast — all were draining me of stamina and strength. I felt that I must have relief; I felt that I must have food.

My promise to fast until Britney ate appeared impossible to keep. As long as she was unconscious, Britney could not eat; she would be fed intravenously. Dr. Barnett still offered no hope of her regaining consciousness. The most promising prediction was that Britney could be in a coma for at least six months and then she would likely be a human vegetable the rest of her life.

As days passed and Britney remained comatose, the pressure mounted on me to eat. Most of my family were disturbed; some were even angry with me. Friends and relatives brought food as they tried to persuade me to eat. Nurses exhorted me by explaining that I would need my strength to be of benefit to Britney if and when she regained consciousness. Mike complained of my loss of weight and strength, of my ability to continue fighting without eating.

So, on the ninth day, I asked God if He wanted me to end

the fast. I went to His Word for my answer. The Bible fell open to the gospel of John; my eyes rested on the 31st verse of chapter 4. As if God Himself were speaking, the words leaped out:

"In the meanwhile his disciples prayed him, saying, Master, eat. But he said unto them, I have meat to eat that ye know not of. Therefore said the disciples one to another, Hath any man brought him anything to eat? Jesus saith unto them, My meat is to do the will of him that sent me, and to finish his word" vv. 31-34).

I had my answer from God. As Christ was being sustained by something more nutritious than food — the will of His Father — so, also, was I. His Word, which I devoured, would be my strength and it was sufficient. Firmly convinced that I was doing God's will, I continued to fast.

The same day that I renewed my commitment to fast, God began moving on my behalf. The likelihood of my being able to eat increased because Britney was taken off the critical list as she moved into a semi-comatose state. Although the change was barely noticeable at first, we were encouraged by the slight improvement.

We had been told that patients don't suddenly wake up from a coma and act as if nothing ever happened, but we wanted Britney to do something now that she had become semi-comatose. For hours we talked to her hoping that, by chance, we would suddenly revive her.

Evidently we said something right because on day nine we elicited a response from Britney. She didn't speak or open her eyes; she smiled! We didn't even know what we said that reached her, but she smiled at us.

We were estatic! Who would have thought that one little smile could produce such a release from pent-up emotions?

Britney's smile was just one of several miracles in which she responded to an outside stimulus. Her first act was to communicate with Mike. His oft repeated question, "If you can hear me, raise one finger," finally elicited a response on the tenth day; Britney slowly raised the index finger on her left hand. "Do you know this is Daddy?" Again the little finger raised in affirmation to Mike's question.

Others tried to reach Britney, but each one failed. Nurses' pleas fell on deaf ears. Even my questions failed to raise a finger. Mike's voice was apparently the only one penetrating to her subconscious. Mike thought this was wonderful; he felt he was her guardian and her link to the outside world.

I, too, had special moments with Britney. Her tiny hand clasped in mine, I'd sit beside her bed and sing. Evidently, Britney liked this because one day when I stopped singing, her fingers tightened around mine as to say, "More, Mommy." When I started singing again, her fingers relaxed their grip. This continued until I could hardly sing another note, but I wouldn't refuse her request. As I sang, tears filled my eyes. Just the thought of Britney communicating with me even though she was semi-comatose caused my heart to overflow with joy.

There would be more testing but for now God was providing comfort in the midst of our tribulation.

8

The Battle Resumes

During our break from the perpetual oppression, our spirits were lifted and thank God they were, for on day ten we were besieged by another adversary — the formation of thousands of blood clots inside Britney's head. The nurses would place hot pads around her head to soften the unwanted particles of blood. Then they would insert syringes under her skull and up inside her head to draw the clots out. This was a horrible procedure and one that we hated, but we knew Britney's brain must be protected from further damage.

The danger to Britney's life presented by the blood clots sent me back to my "refuge," the little hospital chapel. Exhausted, I just lay on the sofa and talked to God for hours. I felt like a child having a "father-daughter" talk. The closeness with God was heart-warming; my Heavenly Father would solve my problems because He understood and because He cared for me. And the love — everlasting love — I felt for Him exuded from the very core of my soul.

From my heart — truthfully and without pretense — I talked to God. "Father, You've done so much already and I'm almost ashamed to ask for more, but where else can I go except to You? You're the only one that Britney and I have. You're our hope, our life, our being. Your Word tells me that in the time of trouble, You're our refuge and our strength and that we can cast our cares upon You because You care for us. Father, Your Word also says, 'Blessed is the man who trusteth in the

Lord, . . . For he shall be like a tree planted by the waters' (Jeremiah 17:7, 8). Well, Father, I'm going to trust You again. In Your Son's name, I'm asking that You remove these blood clots from Britney's head. Take this care from me and be my strength for what lies ahead. Amen."

Hours passed, yet the clots remained. I reflected on the previous healings and asked myself what was different about the blood clots; why weren't they healed instantly? Puzzled by God's apparent hesitancy, I nonetheless waited, fully expecting Him to intervene in His time.

The waiting continued as on the eleventh day, Britney had yet another setback. Along with the blood clots, this latest complication sent Britney from the road to recovery back to the critical list.

Since the surgery, air had been pumped into Britney's lungs via a tube inserted in her mouth. The tube was later placed in her nose and down her throat. This concerned Dr. Sessions because he was afraid the tube would damage her larynx if it remained in her throat too long. He felt it best to perform a tracheotomy and insert the tube through her neck.

I hated even the thought of a tracheotomy; I didn't want Britney's throat cut for any reason. God, however, in His infinite wisdom, had a solution to the problem, and it was a most unusual one.

Several times a day, nurses came and suctioned Britney's lungs — an extremely nauseating procedure to watch. When asked why this was necessary, they explained, "If Britney gets pneumonia, she could die. By drawing the mucous out, we hope to ward off pneumonia."

In spite of their efforts, on day eleven, it happened. I found out late that night when I went down to be with Britney. I opened the door but a nurse suddenly appeared in the doorway blocking my entrance. "You can't come in, Mrs. Foster."

"Why not?" I asked. She offered no explanation. "What's

wrong? Something's happened, hasn't it? I know something's changed!"

"Britney has pneumonia; I'm sorry. We did all we could."

The severity of this development pierced my heart. Not only had the nurses warned us but Dr. Sessions himself had told Mike that if Britney developed pneumonia, she very likely would die. I know there is a better world beyond this one and that God has removed the sting of death for those who love the Lord, but I couldn't bear the thought of my Britney dying.

I hurt and I could hardly think; yet I declared my faith in God to heal Britney — "If there's a God in Israel, she will not have pneumonia. She will live!" That was all I said and why I said it, I don't know.

I must have shocked the nurse because she said nothing. She just nodded her head as if to say, "Uh huh" and closed the door.

As I stood in the hall looking out the window, Satan assailed me, filling my mind with doubt — "Why don't you just jump out this window and kill yourself and it'll all be over? You're not strong enough to go through this!"

Another voice said, "Go pray."

Heeding the call for prayer, I headed for the chapel. There I poured my heart out to God — "Lord, You said I have power over the enemy and that nothing would injure me (Luke 10:17). Well Lord, I don't feel very powerful and I'm hurting! Satan, my enemy, wants to destroy me so I can't stand in the gap for Britney. She has pneumonia and she needs me now more than ever. So, God, I'm going to hold fast to the truth of Your Word. I'm going to believe that greater is He that is in me than he that is in the world (1 John 4:4). In Jesus' name, I'm asking that You deliver me out of Satan's oppressive fear. Amen."

When I finished praying, the Holy Spirit filled my mind with words of encouragement — "God is our refuge and strength, a very present help in trouble" (Psalms 46:1); ". . . Lo, I am with

41

you always even unto the end of the world" (Matthew 28:20). What comfort I took in these Scriptures — what hope they were because God was telling me that He was with me in the present crisis.

I then went back to the family room to join the others. I knew I must tell them of Britney's severe setback but when I walked in, it was apparent that they had already heard the bad news. Saddened faces and red, swollen eyes told it all. Each of them knew, as I did, what this newest complication meant to Britney's chances for survival.

I decided that to withstand another round with the death angel I must follow David's example when he said, "I will encourage myself in the Lord." I walked into the bathroom, knelt down and talked to my Lord — "Father, how much can her little body endure? How much can Mike and I endure? Lord, You said You wouldn't put more on us than we could bear. I thank You, Jesus, for being triumphant, for making intercession for us and for being a High Priest who is touched with the feelings of our infirmities.

"Father, help Mike and me to be like Moses, '. . . for he endured, as seeing him who is invisible' (Hebrews 11:27). Don't let me go by what I see; help me to look to You, 'the author and finisher of my faith.'

"Lord, You said all we have to do is ask. That's what I'm doing. I'm asking for Britney to be healed of pneumonia. Heal her of pneumonia, heal her brain, heal her right side. That's all I can say as Your child. I'm asking in faith in Jesus' name. Amen."

After the prayer, I felt relieved and strengthened. God had lifted my burden and removed my heavy load. Britney's having pneumonia no longer sent waves of fear through my body because I felt that God had heard my prayer.

Upon reentering the family room, I tried to console the others but everyone ignored me. My irrational statements confirmed their fears that I, indeed, had gone off the deep end.

The pressure of Britney's battle with death and my fasting for eleven days must surely have gotten the best of me. How could I think Britney was going to be all right? She had pneumonia!

Mike was particularly upset because he felt this was the end; Britney would die this time. Not wanting to leave her for a moment, he stood beside her bed for hours whispering in her

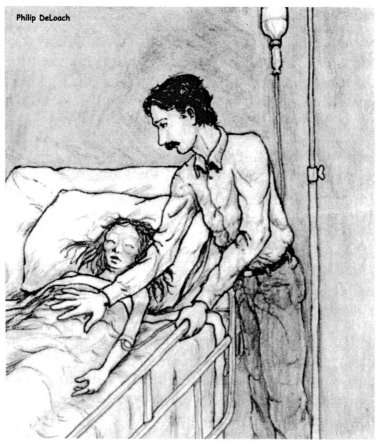

Philip DeLoach

ear. "Daddy's here and you're going to be all right."

Around three o'clock we finally gave up from sheer exhaustion and lay down in the family room. We managed to doze for only a couple of hours because the ringing of the telephone woke us up. Startled and half asleep, Mike answered. An ICU nurse had news for us — "Dr. Sessions would like to see you and Mrs. Foster at once down at Britney's room."

Dr. Sessions had told Mike earlier that he would not ask to speak to us unless Britney's condition was either a great deal better or a great deal worse. Fear gripped Mike as he assumed the worst; he thought Britney was dead. I started to be afraid too, but the Holy Spirit spoke to my heart, "This will be a good report."

As we approached Britney's room, a tall, thin doctor stood in the hall beside her door. "That's Dr. Sessions," Mike whispered. He leaned against the wall with his head drooped over. He amused himself with the patting motion of his foot.

Fighting to restrain the tears, Mike asked, "What is it, Dr. Sessions? What's wrong?"

Ignoring Mike, Dr. Sessions looked at me instead. "Are you Mrs. Foster?"

"Yes I am."

"I was beginning to think Britney didn't have a mother." He hadn't met me because I was usually in the prayer room when he made his rounds.

"I've spent a good bit of my time in the prayer room praying for Britney."

Dr. Sessions came right to the point. "I've got a good report for you. Britney has taken a turn for the better. The pneumonia is gone and her lungs are now functioning properly. In a couple of days we'll take her off the respirator. You realize, of course, that this means we won't have to perform the tracheotomy either."

When I raised my hands to praise God, Dr. Sessions quickly turned away and started talking to Mike. I continued to thank God in my heart because once again He had brought blessing out of crisis. Overnight, Britney's pneumonia was gone, her lungs were better than ever and the dreaded tracheotomy was avoided. God had intervened again in what appeared to be an impossible situation and showed, as He had so many times before, that with Him nothing is impossible.

On the afternoon of day twelve, God moved again. When I went in to see Britney, the day nurse was beaming. "Mrs. Foster, I have more good news. The blood clots in your daughter's head are gone!"

God had moved another mountain; Britney had survived yet another crisis. Once again, when she needed a supernatural touch, God had responded by healing her.

Britney still was not well by any means, but it now appeared that she would live; death, our ever-present enemy, had apparently been defeated. It was only a matter of time — we hoped — before she regained full consciousness. Surely, God would bless us with this great miracle; He had already done so much.

9

God Remembered Us

Nothing can blot the memory of man from God's mind. And when God remembers man, He often employs a gradual process to solve his problems. His treatment of Noah and Elijah are classic examples of these great truths.

God led Noah into the ark of safety for his own salvation. But during his year afloat, Noah could easily have thought that God had forgotten him and his desire to be back to a normal way of life on dry land. With the storms raging outside, Noah had to have faith that God would remember him. And He did: "And God remembered Noah" (Genesis 8:1).

God then began drying up the land after the rain had ceased. As the waters receded, Noah monitored the drying process by sending out a raven and then a dove which showed that everything was gradually being worked out by God.

God answered Elijah's prayers in much the same way when He sent rain after a three-year drought. It appeared that God had forgotten the tiny nation of Israel until He promised Elijah there would be rain.

Elijah believed God's promise and prophesied accordingly. As Elijah prophesied, there was a great rain, but it came as a process and not as an instantaneous response to Elijah's prayers. The process began when the little cloud like a man's hand arose from the sea, Elijah's sign that rain would follow. It confirmed his faith and reassured him that God had not forgotten His promise.

Our deliverance is not always instantaneous either. At times, God solves our problems through a gradual step-by-step process. But when the eyes of faith sees God beginning to work, the child of God can rejoice and wait with assurance for complete deliverance.

When God begins to move in our lives, He often sends indication that our problems are being worked out according to His purpose. Noah knew it when the dove returned with an olive leaf, and Elijah knew it when his servant saw a little cloud like a man's hand. And we were given hope for Britney's complete deliverance when God began sending indicators to us that the healing process had begun.

On the twelfth day, Britney was at a turning point. She remained semi-comatose, but after God healed her of pneumonia and blood clots in her head, Britney's condition took a decided turn for the better. Particularly encouraging were her smiles; smiles which were a prelude to the blessings to follow. The smiles, oddly enough, resulted from a missing tooth. One of Britney's front teeth had been accidentally knocked out when the respirator tube was removed from her mouth and placed in her nose. However, she didn't seem to mind. She'd dart her tongue in and out of the hole created by the missing tooth and then grin sheepishly.

Britney's reaction encouraged us because it meant that her sense of awareness was growing keener. And it was our hope — our indicator — that she would recover from her comatose condition.

On day thirteen, the life support system was removed as Britney's condition improved and her lungs began functioning on their own.

Day fourteen was a day of excitement and thanksgiving. I was anxious to see Britney that morning because for two days, her condition had improved dramatically. "This will be a day to remember," I thought as I hurriedly walked down the hall toward her room. A smiling nurse greeted me as I eased Britney's door open. "Mrs. Foster, I have wonderful news; Britney just woke up!"

Through eyes that remained swollen almost shut, she stared straight ahead. Britney didn't speak or move any more than usual, but she nodded her head when I asked her questions — something she hadn't done before. Her period of awareness was short-lived, though, as she drifted back to sleep and slept all that day.

But before she did, Britney ate, and I was allowed to feed her. After each spoonful of Jello or broth she'd open her mouth like a hungry little bird pleading for more. Except for the couple of bites I took, Britney consumed every morsel.

While Britney ate, I praised God. "Father, I love You. I adore You. I worship You." Praise fell from my lips continuously. God's love seemed to bathe my soul, my mind, my entire being. No amount of money, no, not every world in the galaxy could have purchased from me the feeling of ecstasy I experienced as I watched her eat. The thought of God allowing me, and no one else, to share with Britney her first meal was overwhelming.

God has a perfect order for everything.

Britney's eating again was a miracle, a miracle just as precious and wonderful as all the others God had already performed. It was more than food being eaten by a child. It was the renewal of life after fourteen days of death; fourteen days in which I had seen Britney lie with only a trace of life, with no promise of coming out of a coma. It was my added assurance that our baby was on her way to recovery.

I had kept my commitment to "not eat a bite of food until I eat with Britney" and God honored that commitment. As He promised in His Word (Matthew 6:17, 18), God rewarded me by intervening and prevailing in each crisis and against every obstacle. Because He did, Britney didn't die. (Her condition had been considered one of the most critical of all the patients in the ICU but, ironically, she was spared while five others died.) Because He did, Britney was miraculously healed many times. Because He did, Britney didn't remain comatose for six months. Because He did, I could eat again.

Fasting is a strong ally of the child of God. Even so, I hesitate to recommend that others fast for the healing of their loved ones — that's a personal thing. I didn't feel that fasting was a requirement for Britney's healing, but I do believe it showed God how serious I was about that healing and how much I believed in Him to sustain me. He honored that.

Britney didn't become totally coherent for several more days. She continued to wake up, stare at us, and then quietly slip off to sleep. Because of her weakness, her activities were limited to nodding her head, raising her fingers (on the left hand), and squeezing our hands when we asked her questions.

Gradually, Britney began to speak. At first, she said only a word or two. Then, because she was eating again, her strength increased daily and she began talking more. Soon, she was speaking complete sentences.

She became inquisitive, too. One day, in a deep, gruff voice (the respirator tube had damaged her throat and larynx), she asked, "Mommy, what happened?" Britney didn't realize she was in the Intensive Care Unit at Kennestone Hospital, and she showed no signs of remembering the accident.

"You've been hurt, Darling, but everything's going to be all right." She accepted my simple explanation without further question.

Britney talked, but she became very imitative. I'd say, "Britney, how are you today?" She'd respond, "Britney, how are you today?" To, "Britney, what do you want to eat?" She'd reply, "Britney, what do you want to eat?"

Then to our surprise, Britney began singing. Her song was like her sentences — repetitious. Time after time she sang "Happy Birthday" — a phenomenon for which we had no explanation.

She wanted me to sing too. My having sung to her while she was comatose must have made an impact on her subconscious because now she wanted an encore. "Sing, Mama. Sing to me," she begged.

At first, Britney had lapses of memory as part of her brain continued to sleep. Then after several days, her memory improved. She even related the accident to me, much to my surprise. Her reasoning power improved and she stopped fading back and forth between alertness and incoherence.

To be alive seemed to bring total contentment to Britney. She grinned a lot and, at times, laughed at even the driest of remarks, particularly her own.

The glow on Britney's face was an outward expression of the peace she had in her heart. This peace I attribute in part to an experience she had while in a coma. One day, for no reason, Britney asked, "Mother, did you see that angel?"

Thinking that she meant there with us, I scanned the room. Seeing nothing, I asked her where.

"Not here, Mother. When I was in my long sleep." Long sleep was Britney's definition of coma.

"No, I didn't. How did it look?"

"Well, I saw two angels."

"You did." I was amazed because Britney was very serious.

"Yeah. The first one came and stood on this side of the bed." Britney pointed to her left side.

"He had on this long black robe and a black hood over his head. He was so ugly, Mother. He kept calling my name, 'Britney, Britney' in the most scary voice. He kept trying to grab my hand too. He was so frightening looking, Mother. I was too afraid to open my eyes so I looked at him like this." Britney squinted her eyes.

"I looked up and Jesus was standing there. He told that

one [meaning the black-robed individual], 'You come up here' and He told another one, 'You go down there and be with her.' Mommy, He sent me the cutest little angel."

"How did it look?"

"Mommy, he was so little. He had wings on his back and curly golden hair. He flew down and sat beside my bed and started playing music on his harp. It was the most beautiful music, Mother.

"He never left me. It made me feel good that he was there, but I got tired of him being right beside me all the time so I got up and walked away from him. I hid behind a tree, but he just followed me and stayed right there with me. I finally went back to my bed and lay down. He went back with me and sat down. He stayed with me the whole time I was in my long sleep.

"Mother, most of the time he played music on his harp. But, one time, he stopped and told me something kinda strange. He reached over and patted my hand and said, 'Britney, you're gonna go to heaven, but when you go, you'll be alive.'"

When it appeared for certain that Britney would die, I had asked God to take away the death angel and send her a ministering angel. God answered the prayer, but what I had imagined to be a huge angel at Britney's door had been a tiny angel who remained by her bedside. God had taken the hooded, black thing and sent Britney a cute, curly-haired companion to be with her during her "long sleep."

Britney's angelic visit was a real experience for her. Undoubtedly, it contributed to her exuberance and praise one day when Mother and I were talking about the goodness of God. Mother walked to Britney's bedside and took her hand. "Britney, you know that the Lord loves you and that He's going to completely heal you, don't you?"

"I know it. I know it. Thank You, Jesus. I do believe it." Britney's response melted our hearts as the warmth of the presence of God filled the room. Marble-sized tears flowed

from swollen and darkened eyes, down puffy cheeks and onto her pillow. Her frail left arm raised slowly toward heaven. As her strength waned, the arm fell with a thump to the bed. But then the power of the love in her heart flowed into her arm and up it went again as she magnified God. "I love You, Jesus. I love You, Jesus."

Mother and I rejoiced. I was touched to the core of my soul at seeing her feeble arm, wavering as a wind-blown branch, raised as an expression of the love she felt in her heart for the living God of the universe. Mother offered additional encouragement — "The Lord will honor your faith, Britney, and He'll honor you for praising Him. You just rest in that and know that the Lord is always with you."

For Britney to possess such love and faith and to praise God in her condition, I know the Lord had to be with her and she had had an experience with Him. Britney's praise was her way of telling God she was going to love Him and trust Him in spite of what had happened and in spite of her condition. Her actions proclaimed as did Job, "Though he slay me, yet will I hope in him" (Job 13:15). Together we had walked through the valley of the shadow of death. Together we were sharing the blessings of God. Our sorrow had now turned to joy.

* * * *

Britney remained in the ICU three days after coming out of a coma. Her condition stabilized and she was moved to the Children's Wing. For her miraculous recovery and gradual improvement, we rejoiced.

But as we did, Britney suffered a disheartening setback — another bladder-related disorder. Since her first day in the hospital, Britney had been catheterized. Weeks passed and still the catheter remained in place. This concerned me because I imagined how uncomfortable and even painful this was to Britney. In spite of my numerous requests for the catheter to be removed, the nurses always insisted that it remain in place.

One night, Britney woke up crying. Holding her stomach, she rolled in bed as tears flowed from half-opened eyes. "My stomach, my stomach. It hurts so bad, Mommy!"

Attributing her pain to prolonged use of the catheter, I was now determined that it had to be removed. I ran into the hall and pleaded with the first nurse I saw. "Nurse, you've got to remove this catheter. It's causing her terrible pain."

"Mrs. Foster, you've got to understand, Britney has no control over her bladder and bowels right now. That's going to take rehabilitation. She'll have to be taught to void on her own all over again. The catheter's been in so long that she's lost the sensation. Even if the feeling of fullness comes back, Britney will not be able to control her bladder for a very long while. We don't even know if she ever will."

I tried to console myself, but when I returned to Britney's room she was rolling and sobbing again. Mistee and Mike were doing their best to comfort her, but to no avail. Sensing the futility of our own efforts, I grabbed Mistee's hand and pulled her toward the door. "Come on, Mistee. Let's go to the prayer room."

There, I reached out to God. "Lord, I'm going to let Mistee stand in for her sister. I'm going to lay my hands on her and ask You in the name of Jesus Christ to remove that catheter. You know and I know she can't take this pain. You can remove that catheter and You can heal her bladder. I'm asking You for this miracle in Jesus' name. Amen."

When we returned to Britney's room, she wasn't in her bed, and Mike was gone. As I turned to leave, I saw them, but I could hardly believe my eyes; Britney was on the commode slouched over like a little Raggedy Ann. Mike was behind her nervously holding her limp body erect.

"They told me to start sitting her on the commode because the legs sometimes get a certain feeling that way. Those feelings could spark the memory of voiding."

Then I saw it; the catheter, covered with pus and blood, dangled between Britney's legs. Adhesive tape, attaching it to her leg, prevented the catheter from falling to the floor.

"Mike, did you pull that catheter out? You have pulled this catheter out!"

He defended himself. "No, I didn't. I haven't touched it."

"Britney, did you pull that out?"

"No, Mommy. I wouldn't do that."

Britney had tossed in her bed for weeks and had been taken from her bed to the bathtub numerous times. But the catheter hadn't come out — until now.

"Mike, this is another miracle! God removed that catheter!" I cried and laughed at the same time; God had moved so quickly. Praise to the one that, when He works, nothing hinders. How wonderful He is and how powerful is His Word.

"Sherry, you know the nurses will put it back," Mike cautioned as he lay Britney back on her bed.

"No, they're not! The Lord removed that catheter, and they're not going to put it back. You saw the pus and blood!"

I was afraid not to tell the duty nurse about the catheter, but when I did, she fumed. "Mrs. Foster, did you pull it out?"

"No, ma'am, I didn't. I prayed for God to remove the catheter, and I truly believe that's how it happened — God removed it."

"Well, you know we'll have to put it right back in."

"Please give her a chance. Just let her have 'til morning to void on her own."

She looked at me. I held my breath. "Four hours. If she hasn't voided by then, we'll have to put the catheter back in."

Britney needed prayer. Though time was of the essence, I took Mistee and drove to Mother's church about sixty miles away. We interrupted Wednesday night prayer service long enough to ask the church members to lay hands on Mistee on behalf of her sister and pray that God would let Britney void on her own.

As I drove back to Kennestone, thoughts of the many times God had already healed Britney increased my faith. I dared not question His willingness to manifest His love once again when He had blessed us so many times before. The same duty nurse greeted us at Britney's door. "Mrs. Foster, you'll be pleased to know that your daughter voided on her own while you were gone."

My joy erupted into praise.

"Now, that doesn't necessarily mean we can keep the catheter out. I'm sure Britney doesn't have any sensation or control over her bladder. There's no way she can know when to void. She'll just wet the bed."

"I'd rather she wet the bed. Just give her time. Please let it stay out a little longer."

She finally gave in. "Tomorrow. We'll give her until tomorrow." For the slight reprieve, I whispered a prayer of thanksgiving.

By then, it was past midnight and Mistee had gone home

with Mike's mother. Exhausted, Mike and I fell asleep in our all-too-familiar positions — beside Britney's bed.

Around five o'clock, a low, soft voice awakened me. "Mommy, Mommy. I've got to pee pee." I was ecstatic when she voided on her own and the nurses were thoroughly amazed. They still didn't realize that we were relying on "The Great Physician" to restore our child's health. It was He who had removed the catheter and restored lost sensations and bladder control. Praise, glory, and honor to His holy name. I love Him so much and praise Him because He is a prayer-answering God.

*   *   *   *

Britney had moved her right leg a little, but her right arm and hand were completely paralyzed. No matter what we did to stimulate the arm — moving it up and down, stroking it, even pinching it — it lay limp and lifeless.

One day, in the special therapy room, I asked the therapist if she had any hope of Britney ever regaining the use of her right arm. "No ma'am, I don't. Her arm may always hang by her side — useless." After showing me a picture of the cerebellum and explaining that it controlled the motor functions of the body, she elaborated further, "Mrs. Foster, you've got to understand that part of Britney's cerebellum was removed. What wasn't removed was penetrated by bone and severely traumatized by the impact of the blow to her head. To make matters worse, she had a huge blood clot on her brain that starved many of the cells around it."

"What, then, will she be able to do?"

"She may regain some feelings in her arm in time, but she'll never be able to use her fingers; she'll have absolutely no dexterity in them. With therapy, she might be able to move her arm through action of her shoulder muscles much like a quadriplegic does."

I couldn't accept that. "God doesn't lead us to the Red Sea

and then not part it. He hasn't brought Britney this far to let her be paralyzed the rest of her life. I don't accept that. I'll not have it."

"Well, Mrs. Foster, there's nothing you can do about it."

"You're right! I can't, but I know one that can!"

With that, I sat Britney in her wheelchair and pushed her back to her room. As I did, I talked to God. "Lord, I don't believe this. I'll not accept this useless report. We've seen one healing after another and now we need You again. You created Britney's cerebellum and You can certainly heal it, even if it means creating another."

When we returned to Britney's room, I cried for hours. I knew that God was able and more than willing to do the impossible again, but the discouraging report broke my heart. Mike, disturbed too, tried to console me until his tired body refused to function any longer and he fell asleep.

Britney and I were denied the luxury — we couldn't sleep. As I looked at my baby, I knew how her heart must hurt. So I prayed again. "God, I don't believe this. You said that when You started a work, You finished it. I can't believe it, Lord. Please heal her right arm and fingers."

Suddenly, and without warning, a voice from behind startled me: "Read my Word to her because it is health to all your flesh." Although the voice seemed at a distance, it was strong and so real that I turned in my chair to see who was there. I saw no one.

Assured that God Himself had visited me and had pronounced health on Britney, I turned to the book of Matthew and read aloud three chapters to which Britney fell sound asleep. I thought, 'What will God do next? How will He again show us that He has remembered us?' His presence continued to flood the room as I, too, fell asleep.

God was working elsewhere as we slept; He was dealing with Mother at her home. Mother is always in close communion

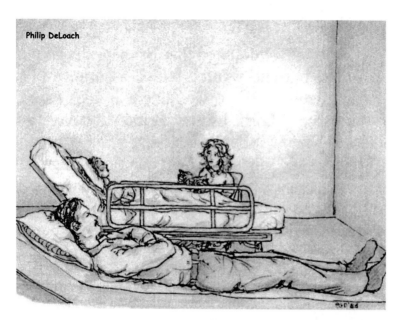

Philip DeLoach

with God but, on this occasion, His presence was particularly real and meaningful. God dealt with her in much the same way that He dealt with Abraham when he asked God for a sign.

Abraham "believed in the Lord; and he counted it to him for righteousness" (Genesis 15:6). Abraham had faith that God would fulfill His promise of a great nation. Yet, he asked for a sign (Genesis 15:8), not that he doubted, but because he wanted confirmation and assurance. And the Lord responded (Genesis 15:9-17).

Mother never doubted that Britney was going to be healed but she wanted added assurance. That morning, she talked to God like she does early in the morning. "Lord, I know Britney's going to be all right. I know it because You've already brought her through so much and You don't do things halfway. But I'm exhausted, Lord. So, just for my sake, will You give me a sign? I'm not asking for a sign to believe because I already believe. I need something just to comfort me so my mind can rest a little bit."

When Mother said that, God spoke to her too. "You remember when Elijah sent his servant out to see if there was a cloud in the sky?"

"Yes, Sir."

"Well, when he went back the seventh time, he saw a cloud like a man's hand. That was his sign that rain would fall on Israel. Britney will move her right thumb and that will be your sign!"

God moved swiftly as we saw when Britney awoke. Mike and I were still asleep when Britney whispered, "Mommy, Mommy! Wake up!"

I lifted my head and leaned forward in my chair to see what she wanted. Britney beamed and pointed toward her right hand with her left. The thumb was moving just as God had promised Mother. Joy welled up inside me. "Britney, you moved your thumb! Make it move again!" She did. "Mike, get up! Britney's moved her thumb!"

Mike awakened and with uncontrolled exuberance, leaped over Britney's bed as if he were spring-loaded. "Britney, move it for Daddy! Move it for Daddy! Let me see you do it!" When she did, we all cried with inexplicable delight. Now that the process had begun, Mike was ready for more. "Can you move your fingers? Let me see you move your fingers." Again she responded; one at a time the little fingers wiggled.

The more we requested, the more she did. We asked her to open her hand and she did. Mike then asked her to raise her arm. And, with extreme difficulty, she did. Then, because it was so weak, her arm flopped back on the bed. But, at least, it was no longer dead; her arm had moved — nothing less than another miracle.

I praised the Lord and Mike cried. Some of the nurses cried too. Britney was exuberant as tears ran down her face. "Mommy, I moved my fingers! I moved my arm!" Radiating from her face were hope, release from fear, a look of sheer ecstasy — a look I had long waited for.

When Mother called later that morning, my first words to her were, "Guess what just happened?"

Confidently, she answered, "I know what happened. Britney's moved her right thumb." The telephone wires were charged as Mother and I explained to each other what God had said. We rejoiced not only because God had spoken to us, but because He had allowed us to share this miracle even though we were miles apart.

God healed Britney in spite of the therapist's prediction. What was considered by some to be a physical impossibility had taken place. Britney had moved parts of her body that had been dormant for weeks and, because of the damage to the control center of her brain, were supposed to remain that way. Truly, God's Word is health to our flesh.

As Britney's smiles had been an indication to us that she would totally recover from her comatose condition, the slight movement of her right thumb was our sign that she would be totally and miraculously healed of all the predicted handicaps. We could now be confident that the process had begun — a process that when complete would restore Britney to her rightful place as a healthy young girl.

10

The Valley of Depression

Although the healing process had begun, before it re-
sumed, we were to go through a period of severe mental
anguish. When God remembered and blessed us, apparently
He had also been preparing us for the dreary days ahead — a
time in which our spirits plummetted to an all-time low in the
valley of depression.

After a week in the Children's Wing, Britney was moved to
Rehabilitation. Pleased with her progress, I continued to hold
fast to my trust in God that, whether by therapeutic means or
by divine intervention, He would restore to Britney the quality
of life she had known before the accident.

In spite of her progress, Britney was far from normal. She
had lost movements many of us take for granted. She couldn't
even sit up in bed. She could move her right leg, but movements were spastic and difficult. Her head, which remained
swollen and heavy, wobbled and bobbed up and down as her
eyes wandered aimlessly, unable to focus. Yet, Britney didn't
complain; she had hope.

Our hopes for normalcy through therapy were dashed by
Britney's therapist shortly after she arrived in Rehabilitation.
The therapist was quick to point out that even though Britney
had moved her arm and fingers, she would never have complete use of them. If she walked again, she would have ataxia
(loss of the power of muscular coordination). The therapist

also expressed concern that the blow to the front of Britney's head had damaged the area of her brain that controls speech and memory — a speech impediment and loss of memory could result.

My constant vigil for Britney, the fourteen-day fast, and my struggle to overcome fear and oppression had taken their toll — my strength and resistance were almost gone. Walking was a chore and bathing became drudgery; just to get into the shower and stand was a challenge. The healing process had begun in the Children's Wing — of this I was sure — and I wanted to trust God. But, in my weakened state, the odds looked insurmountable and I didn't know how much fight remained in me.

Mike had gone back to work when Britney was moved to Rehabilitation so I was left to fight alone. Because his job was out of town, we only saw him on weekends. This in itself was demoralizing, but I realized more than ever how much Britney needed him. He had a special way with her and she missed him a lot.

Weakened, and confronted by Britney's severe handicaps, I found myself filled with despair — depression became a mortal enemy. This new adversary caught me off guard because I had relaxed a bit in the Children's Wing. Britney seemed better so I thought the worst was over, that there would be no more fighting. I was wrong. This time, however, the battleground was within, and the battle was with a state of mind, with an unwanted feeling, with depression itself.

Each night, I welcomed the end of a dreary day. I'd collapse on my cot and pray for strength for the next day — strength I sorely needed because my nerves were frayed. Somehow, by repeating, "Lo, I am with you always even until the end of the world," I felt comfort. I kept my sanity.

My despair was aggravated by the conditions under which I had lived since the accident. During those 2-1/2 months, I had gone home only once; I remained with Britney. Normal daily activities had long since vanished, so time, as I had known it, ceased to exist. Days blended together and became as one long, unforgettable day.

I felt as if I were imprisoned in Kennestone. I'd look out the window at people going by in their cars. To myself, I'd complain, "I'll never get out there again and go as I please. These walls have become my prison — my spotless, stainless steel prison." The coldness of the hospital made me feel as if I were in solitary confinement. And I was being punished by having to listen to the click, click, click of passing wheelchairs and the squeaking of the elevator day after day.

As a prisoner, I yearned to be on the outside. I wanted to be free of the vise that had gripped my life. I wanted to be free of the strict hospital rules which had, for weeks, dictated my every move. I wanted my own bed.

Britney wasn't free either. Other patients came and went back home while she remained. I'd look at the grass and the trees and recall how she once ran outside, how she loved to go on picnics and to Six Flags. Britney loved life and now here she lay, imprisoned by her own inability to do the things she once loved to do. "Get up, Britney. Let's go home," I wanted to say. We weren't where we should be and I wanted to go home. My wishes were not granted, however, and imprisoned we remained.

But, when we find ourselves bound and in need of God's assurance, He reaches down and touches us. His touch is timely. His touch is gentle. His touch is simple, yet profound. His touch is strength anew so that once again we can begin the battle of faith. His touch is a reminder that the giving and taking of life is His prerogative and His alone. His touch is our assurance that the care and concern He has for His children exceeds even that which we have for our own children. His touch is love — boundless love; love that sets the captive free.

I began to think of the ways God had proven His love. Giving His only begotten Son for our sins was the ultimate expression of God's love. His love was again manifest when the Son took the stripes on His back for our healing. And it was that same love that had on numerous occasions already healed Britney.

Although the job started by God was not yet complete, I felt that He would finish it. God doesn't partially do things; He would finish it. God doesn't partially do things; He doesn't lead us to the Red Sea and then not part it. He would part our Red Sea and Britney would walk through to the other side. There she would have no loss of memory, no speech impediment, no ataxia, full use of her right arm and right leg. Britney would be normal again! In spite of the odds and the overwhelming depression, I was now determined to trust God for her complete healing.

Through these thoughts, God touched me. His reassurance came as Britney and I found ourselves confronted with yet another foe — the depressing conditions in Rehabilitation. According to hospital policy, Britney was to eat with the other therapy patients — mostly stroke victims — in a little dining room at the end of the hall. So, on her first day in Rehabilitation, I placed her in a wheelchair and pushed her down the hall where we would have lunch.

Upon entering the dining room, we were overwhelmed by a morbid feeling. Sitting around small tables attempting to eat were elderly people — mostly men — crying and moaning. Some even drooled. One grey-haired man, who was totally disabled, just sat partially slumped over staring at us. He didn't eat. He just stared with ghostly, yet penetrating, eyes.

Britney dropped her head and started crying. She couldn't eat under these conditions. In less than a minute, we were in front of the nurses' station. "Britney can't eat in there! It's hard enough on her as it is. I just don't think a seven-year-old should have to cope with this too. I can't myself — how can I expect her to?"

The head nurse peered over the top of her glasses. "Mrs. Foster, I'm sorry but it's hospital policy that all therapy patients eat together and your daughter has to abide by the rules."

Thank God it was Friday and Mike would be with us soon; he could straighten everything out. When he arrived, late that afternoon, the other patients were having dinner, so Mike observed the situation first hand. He agreed with me — Britney should not be subjected to that. Neither of us was disdainful of the other patients, but we both maintained that a seven-year-old, already depressed by her own handicap, should not be unnecessarily exposed to more misery. Mike took our case to the head nurse and, with his remarkable power of persuasion, won his argument. As a result, Britney was permitted to eat in the cafeteria with her family — a situation which, I felt, was more conductive to her speedy recovery.

Even so, she remained downcast; Britney was so despondent that I felt compelled to stay with her all night as I had done in the ICU and in the Children's Wing. Mike and the girls needed me, but I felt Britney needed me more.

My decision to stay with her met with strong opposition. The same head nurse who had insisted that Britney eat with the other patients took me aside one day. "Don't you think it's about time for you to start leaving Britney at night so she can adapt to her environment and get accustomed to being alone?" Her constant exposure to sickness had apparently made her somewhat insensitive to the feelings of others.

"Don't even consider that!" I argued. "You're a mother. Would you leave your child up here in this awful place with all these sick people? Would you leave her if she were very sick and scared of being left alone?"

"Yes, I would. I'm a nurse."

"I don't believe that! You can't tell me that because you

67

haven't been in this situation. You don't know what you'd do in my position."

"Britney won't recover as well with you here all the time. You're not being a good mother by being so protective of her."

"I want to be here praying for my daughter and holding her up before God. I believe He brought Britney this far, and I'm trusting Him to completely heal her. And I'm staying here with her even if I have to sleep on the floor!"

She left, but not long after she did, another nurse came to Britney's room and told me that the hospital psychiatrist wanted to see me.

I knew that many of the hospital staff thought I was a little crazy because, in every critical situation, I turned to God for the solution. They couldn't understand why I would run to the chapel, pray, and then insist that God was going to heal my daughter.

To the non-believer, trusting God is an unreasonable approach to problem solving. Those who do trust God are frequently accused of exhibiting irrational behavior because they refuse to rely completely on natural means for the resolution of their problems.

My constant insistence on the power of God to reverse the irreversible, my over-protectiveness of Britney, and finally my refusal to leave her alone at night earned me an invitation to see the hospital psychiatrist. Following some small talk and a few questions about Mike, he came to the point. "Mrs. Foster, your daughter's in good hands here at Kennestone. Why don't you give in a little and let the nurses do what they're paid and trained to do?"

"Because I can do it better. I know her. She's at ease with me."

"Why are you so protective of Britney? Why don't you ever go home?"

"I'm with her because I'm her mother and I love her. I want

to be with her. My place is with my daughter, and I don't care if you do think I should act like she's well and leave her all alone up here. I'm staying with her. My mind is made up!"

"Well, Mrs. Foster, that's your decision. No one can force you to leave; but I would like for you to, at least, accept the reality of your daughter's handicap. In spite of the advances in modern medicine, she may never be normal again. Why are you so insistent on God healing Britney? Why do you think He will?" He paused but when I remained silent, he continued, "Why do you feel that you have to pray for her all the time?"

"I pray for her because that's the way I believe. If you think I'm crazy for not relying solely on medicine, I'm sorry. But my faith and confidence are in God. He's the reason she's alive and I'm trusting Him to completely heal Britney. I firmly believe in the power of God to provide for His own. If you can prove me wrong, I'll believe what you say but, if not, you'll have to believe me!"

Unable to dispute my claims and rather irritated by my unyielding determination, he concluded the session.

As I was leaving, I turned and looked straight at him. "I won't be back. If you want to see me after Britney gets out of the hospital, that'll be fine, but not before. Just leave me alone." I didn't go back and, from that day, nothing more was said about my having to leave Britney alone at night.

I'm glad I held fast to my convictions because, shortly after my confrontation with the psychiatrist, Britney suffered additional emotional unrest. This occurred when, one day, I took her to the special therapy room, thinking nothing of the mirrors that covered all four walls. Placed there, of course, for therapeutic reasons, the mirrors proved to be of no benefit to my little girl that day.

I had just placed Britney on the thick mat in the middle of the floor and turned to close the door when she yelled, "Mommy! Mommy! "

"What is it, baby?" I asked as I ran toward her.

Britney pointed at herself in a mirror. "Who's that, Mommy?" She didn't recognize the disfigured face as her own.

My heart sank; I had failed to prepare Britney for this. Yet, I had to tell her. "It's you Darling."

"Oh, Mommy, what's happened to me? What's wrong with me! Mommy, will I always look like this?"

Britney was frightened; she was looking at something that had been described as inhuman — herself. Her heart was broken and she wept profusely.

Her words pierced my soul but I forced myself to hide the pity I felt for her. "Britney, you'll be okay. All that'll go away."

"I want to get out of here. Take me out of here, Mother. I don't like these mirrors!"

Britney's hopes had vanished so we returned to her room. There was a great deal of work to be done, but it could wait.

Britney's despondency, the negative predictions about her complete recovery and the environment in Rehabilitation could have made me give up. But for Britney's sake, I couldn't; I had to be strong.

No matter how desperate things became for us, I knew that God still loved us and that He would deliver us. I believed that if I waited on Him, He would renew my strength and lift us out of this valley of depression.

"They that wait upon the Lord shall renew their strength; they shall mount up with wings as eagles; they shall run and not be weary; and they shall walk and not faint" (Isaiah 40:31).

11

On the Mountain Top

Unwilling to continue yielding to this tormentor, I determined to personally combat the prevailing feelings of despair. "Britney's room," I thought. "This place needs a facelift. It should be warm, an expression of home away from home."

I went to work. Britney's cold, blank walls became a frame for get-well cards she had received from people all over the United States. We stationed a huge stuffed rabbit beside her bed and filled a tray, which was "held" by the rabbit, with other stuffed animals she had received as gifts.

The new decor cheered us, but nothing like the joy we derived from our favorite pastime — eating. As is the case with most children, Britney loved snacks. Her favorite was potato chips. Before she was hurt, I wouldn't allow her to eat all she wanted because, as a mother, I was anxious for her to eat well-balanced meals; however, my priorities changed when Britney was in a coma. I promised her she could have all the potato chips she wanted if only she would regain consciousness. When she did, I kept my promise. But, instead of feeling disapproval I now felt pleasure to see her devour bag after bag. I just praised God that she could.

Britney enjoyed other snacks, too. Every night she would beg me to bring her chili, popcorn, or crackers with cheese or mayonnaise on them. There were more treats. A big drawer at the base of her closet was our secret hiding place for the goodies she wasn't supposed to eat. In it we kept bananas, apples, and sacks full of candy and bubble gum people had given us. Sometimes, we'd sit on the floor beside the treasure-laden drawer and, as I steadied her, we'd munch like two hamsters while we watched television. It was marvelous seeing her eat real food again — even "junk food."

Britney and I ate so much that I thought we would both be huge. But we had room for growth. Britney had shrunk almost to skin and bones and I had lost fifteen pounds. So, we continued to eat with no thoughts of dieting.

The pleasure we derived from eating was heightened by Britney's continued improvement. The therapist, however, continued to doubt and to look at the circumstances. But I knew that God had set the healing process — an irreversible process — in motion when He allowed Britney to move her fingers and arms. We could have confidence that Britney would be normal again.

For her complete healing, God chose therapeutic treatments — efforts we had been told would be ineffective in Britney's case. But the prayers had been prayed and the process already begun. The therapy would be effective.

But first, I had to persuade Britney to return to the special therapy room. For days she refused to go because it was there she had seen herself in the mirrors. My promise to take her to Six Flags when she was well persuaded her to go the first time.

Although Britney worked hard, and her condition improved daily, the therapist insisted that she would never have full use of her right arm. So, she worked with Britney's left arm as she taught her to put on her clothes and to button her pajamas with the left hand. She also maintained that Britney must learn to write with her left hand and continued her training accordingly.

We tried another approach — we worked with Britney's right arm ourselves. As we did, her writing progressively improved. Because of this improvement and our persistence, the therapist finally conceded and worked with Britney's right arm too. Our diligence paid off; Britney learned to write again with fingers which only days earlier had been pronounced completely and permanently useless. Praise God!

In addition to writing, Britney had to relearn other elementary functions. Like a baby, she was unable to crawl or walk. But she tried hard. In therapy, she worked relentlessly to regain her lost abilities.

I worked with Britney, too, and applauded her as she made improvements. I told her how good she was doing and how proud I was. As she reached another milestone, we laughed together and then waited impatiently until Friday when we would tell her dad.

Britney soon learned to crawl. Then, she could walk a little by holding on to rails.

As usual, the therapist was quick to point out that if Britney ever walked again she would probably have ataxia. She would walk on her toes and bow backward to keep her balance.

However, the therapist was wrong — Britney would not have ataxia. One Saturday when I was in the cafeteria, Mike had taken Britney to the bathroom. But, instead of putting her back in bed, he stood her on the bathroom floor. She grasped the rails on the walls as Mike eased back toward her bed. He then told Britney to take a few steps. She responded by cautiously walking to the end of the rails. But Mike wasn't satisfied. "Now, let go and walk to me."

"Daddy, what if I fall? I can't do this."

"Yes, you can. Just try it for Daddy."

Having not yet walked without support, Britney was afraid and hesitant at first. Then she giggled.

"Okay, I'll try. But catch me if I fall, Daddy."

Britney did let go and she slowly walked toward Mike. She managed a couple of steps before falling into his opened arms. She did it, Britney walked by herself!

They could hardly wait to show me. Like a baby learning to walk, she waddled four or five steps before falling toward Mike. Although she moved slowly, her movements were not spastic, she didn't drag her leg and she didn't walk on her toes. God had performed another miracle — Britney didn't have ataxia.

When Dr. Barnett saw Britney walk normally — with no ataxia, with no limp, and without dragging her right leg — he could offer but one explanation. "I told you I had done all that man could do for your daughter." He pointed up as he continued, "It had to be the man upstairs that did this. I'm amazed at what I've seen. This is truly a miracle!"

Dr. Barnett had used his hands and the knowledge he had gained through years of experience to give Britney every possible chance to live. God had begun His medical wonders where man's ability ceased. When He did, He set into motion a healing process for Britney, a process which began when she miraculously moved her right thumb and progressed until she walked again. Britney was well on the way to full recovery.

12

After the Battle

They may not have agreed with our convictions, but almost everyone in Kennestone Hospital knew about Britney Foster. Her miraculous recovery had attracted a great deal of attention. Even nurses from other floors came to visit. Strangers would stop me in the halls to find out how she was doing and to ask about the miracles. God had performed so many miracles for Britney that she came to be known as "The Miracle Child."

Britney didn't lack for attention either. At first, nobody expected her to live and then, when she did, people were overwhelmed with compassion and love for her. They just couldn't do enough for her. Because it seemed as though she had come back from the dead, everyone wanted to be with Britney and do things for her. Friends and strangers alike came from near and far to visit. She was deluged with gifts too — stuffed animals, games, books, food, flowers and plants, fruit baskets, crayons and coloring books. Each visitor and each gift received the same welcome — Britney's broad grin. Hers was truly a heart of thanksgiving.

People gave money too. Britney's school donated one hundred dollars. The actors and actresses around Atlanta contributed sixteen hundred dollars. I thought things as wonderful as this only happened in the movies. But, thank God, I saw first hand the goodness of my fellow human beings. God was working through them, that by their goodness, His love might be manifested once again.

Britney's friends cared too. Their get-well cards exhibited the innocence and uninhibited love of children. One boy cheered Britney with his assessment of the situation: "Dearest Britney, I'm sitting here in this Kennesaw school thinking about the prettiest girl in class — you. You're like a flower in the springtime. I wish it was spring. I'd go out and fly my kite. And I'd pick you some beautiful flowers because you're the fairest of them all."

After 2-1/2 months of hospitalization, we took Britney home. Following several more months of hard work, she learned to walk again. Then she could run and ride her bike. Soon to follow were roller skates, softball, ballet and gymnastics' classes. For one who was to have difficulty in walking again, she does well in pointing out the beauty of God's miracle.

Now, Britney has fully recovered and her life is back to normal. In spite of the severe swelling to her head, Britney has no problems with her eyes; on the contrary, her vision is perfect. She has never taken any more Dilantin, and she has never had a seizure. Britney carries a ready grin expressive of her love for life and those who share life with her. She is playful, healthy, and intelligent. To God be the glory.

To everyone's amazement, she returned to school on grade level and continued on without interruption.

During her high school years, Britney was vice president of FHA (Future Homemakers of America), on the soccer team, and received the senior superlative for "Friendliest." Britney had proven that God not only spared her life, but restored it completely.

Doctors who learned of Britney's progress were truly astounded. But she didn't stop there. After graduating high school, Britney went on to further her education at Kennesaw State University.

Britney began her college career in September of 1990.

There she majored in Elementary Education. Britney loved children and wanted to play a role in helping to empower them. But only a year later, Britney found another love. *His* name was Chris. Shortly thereafter, in September of 1992, she became the first of the three sisters to wed.

One month before Britney's 21st birthday, she married Christopher Wesley Bowlick. Although there was some speculation that Britney would now end her college career, it never came to pass. She only took one semester off. The true test of Britney's determination to finish school would come in 1995. It was then that she gave birth to a beautiful baby boy — Caleb Matthew. Caleb was an extra special addition to the family because not only was he the first born, but he was also the first grandchild and great grandchild. As you can imagine, he immediately became the center of attention. Now, with this new focus, Britney did decide to take some time off.

After taking a year off, Britney returned to school. The term "college career" had now taken on a whole new meaning for Britney. It was taking a bit longer than she had anticipated; and, being a wife, mother, employee, and college student was quite the juggling act. Naturally, the occasional thought of "postponing" — which really means quitting college — popped up. But realizing she was too close to quit now, Britney pressed on. Britney was only back in school a couple of months when she found out she was pregnant again! Britney wanted another child, yes; but now?

Pregnant with her second child, Britney was unsure of what to do now. She desperately wanted to finish school and become a teacher, but she did not want to neglect her family. Being a wife and mother was not something Britney took lightly. Even though she knew it would pay off in the long run, she feared that the added strain and expense of continuing school now may actually hurt them instead of help them.

After discussing her fears with her husband, the decision

77

was made that Britney would stay in school.

In March of 1997, Leigha Taylor was born. What a joy! And finally, in 1998, Britney graduated! Praise be to God. The one that was not given even half a chance of living by man, God had given a college degree and a family! God is good!

Britney Foster, God's Miracle Child, is a living testimony of God's great love. She is healthy because God in His love supernaturally intervened and because He allowed therapy and the natural healing process to be effective. He can and will answer the prayers of His people.

So if you ever find yourself in an impossible situation, talk to God. Tell Him you know that with Him all things are possible. Search His Word for Scriptures to exercise your faith and speak to your needs. Hold on to your faith, never allowing doubt to enter. Trust Him though all odds may seem against you. And, remember what He did for Britney Foster!

We hope Britney's story has inspired you and helped to build your faith — especially in times of crises. Please write us and let us know if Britney's story helped you in some way or if you asked Jesus to come into your heart as Savior.

Also, if you do not know the Lord Jesus as your Saviour, we hope you will pray this prayer to Him to forgive you and to come into your heart as the Lord of your life — (Read Romans 10:9-13).

Dear Father in heaven — I come to You in the wonderful name of Jesus to ask You to forgive me of all my sins - past - present and future. Wash me clean with Your precious blood You shed for me at Calvary. Come into my heart, change me and help me to live for You for the rest of my life. Thank You, Jesus, that I am now saved and my name is written in the Blood Of Life.

Britney on one of her walks recommended by therapist to build up her right leg.

Britney in front of pool recommended by neurosurgeon and therapist to build up her right side.

Britney as a delegate for the FHA Banquet in Atlanta.

My husband Roy and I have made numerous mission trips to Central and South America. We also co-host Atlanta Live seen on T.V. 57 in Atlanta, Ga. We are involved in ministry outreach here in America. The Lord has given us a heart for all people. Thank you ABBA Father.

Notes:

Notes:

Notes:

Notes:

Notes:

Notes:

Notes:

Notes:

Notes:

_____

_____

_____

_____

_____

_____

_____

_____

_____

_____

_____

_____

_____

_____

_____

_____

_____

_____

_____

_____

_____

_____

_____

Notes:

Notes:

Notes:

_____

_____

_____

_____

_____

_____

_____

_____

_____

_____

_____

_____

_____

_____

_____

_____

_____

_____

_____

_____

_____

_____

CPSIA information can be obtained
at www.ICGtesting.com
Printed in the USA
FSOW02n1111020816
23364FS

9 781449 713669